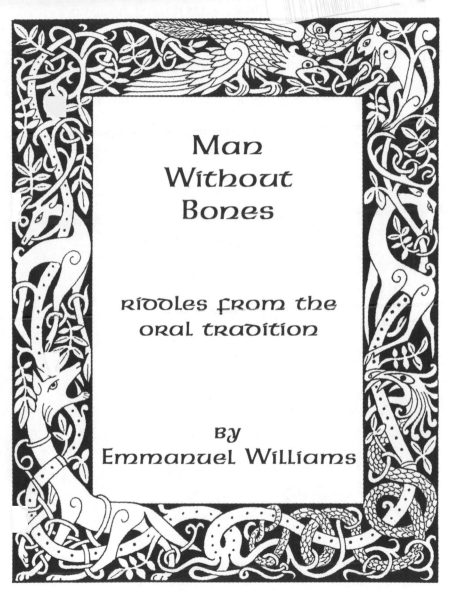

Man Without Bones

Riddles from the oral tradition

By
Emmanuel Williams

Robert D. Reed Publishers
750 La Playa St., Suite 647
San Francisco, CA 94121
Phone: 650-994-6570
Fax: 650-994-6579
E-mail: 4bobreed@msn.com
Web site: www.rdrpublishers.com

Typesetting and Cover Design by:
Dawn Searcy at Graphics Plus in Pacifica, CA

ISBN 1-885003-50-1

Library of Congress Catalog Card No. 00-100652

Produced and Printed in the United States of America

INTRODUCTION

There's something about language games that we love and enjoy. We willingly challenge ourselves with crossword puzzles and word searches; we watch 'Jeopardy' on tv; we play Boggle and Scrabble and Pictionary.

Riddles have been around for thousands of years. I can imagine cavemen staring into the flames of a crackling fire and making them up. Setting the enigma, the puzzle; watching the shaggy eyebrows furrow, the eyes glaze as the mind turns over the possible solutions. The riddler smiles as the puzzle flickers like a bat beyond the mind's grasp. Maybe someone suddenly 'gets' it, and yells it out in triumph, or maybe the silence lengthens into defeat and the riddler prompts discovery with a clue, or takes pity on his or her victims and gives them the solution.

In the Old Testament Creation is accompanied by naming. If we didn't have names for everything we'd find it hard to organize our lives in the world. The price we pay for this is that names get in the way of what they stand for. The symbol obscures, or replaces, reality. Part of the charm - maybe even the magic - of riddles is that they give us a glimpse of the world before everything was identified and classified.

The riddles in this collection are inspired by the Anglo-Saxon Exeter Book of Riddles. (Hence the borders and the fonts we chose.) No one knows who wrote these riddles or when they were written, although it's thought they date from the first half of the eighth century. Most of them were to do with the everyday life of working people - riddles about domestic and work objects, animals, the weather. The Anglo-Saxons were an agricultural people, and the Exeter riddles have been described as 'the song of the unsung laborer.' They always took the form of an object or creature speaking without defining or identifying itself. Sometimes these old riddles were quite raunchy:

I'm a strange creature, for I satisfy women,
a service to the neighbors! No one suffers
at my hands except my slayer.
I grow very tall, erect in a bed,
I'm hairy underneath. From time to time
a good-looking girl, the doughty daughter
of some churl dares to hold me,
grip my russet skin, robs me of my head
and puts me in the pantry. At once that girl
with plaited hair who has confined me
remembers our meeting. Moist is her eye.
(Answer - an onion)

THE SOLUTIONS

There are often a number of different possible solutions to riddles. The riddle quoted below - my grade A hardest one - has had the following solutions suggested: echo, speech, jet plane, thunder, and fart. All of these are, in a sense, right. So if you come up with a solution that's not the same as the one I suggest, and it fits the riddle, bully for you.

WRITING YOUR OWN RIDDLES

As you will see from this collection, there are no particular rules for the form of riddles. I deliberately used a range of poetic techniques - rhyme, repetition, free verse. I think the best riddles are those that work as puzzles, enigmas, AND as poems. A riddle like:

If you can hear
where I come from
I am no longer there

isn't very interesting from the poetic point of view. So aim for success on BOTH fronts - a successful riddle which is also a successful poem.

How do you come up with riddles? Look around you. Look at the objects in your environment and focus on one of them, or allow one of them to impress itself on your consciousness. Could be the TV, or a lamp, or a tree, or a pen, or a belt, or a cloud, or a book, or a cat, or a spoon....Let the object give an account of itself. What would this cup say if it were to speak?

This ring
is for your finger
this lip
is for your mouth.....

and you're away!

Look for riddle subjects that are accessible to people, that aren't too complicated, or personal to you. The riddle that Samson asked the Philistines, for example, was ridiculous:

'Out of the eater came forth meat
and out of the strong came forth sweetness.'

It sounds great but the solution- a honeycomb in the carcass of a dead lion - is inaccessible. The other thing to remember about composing riddles is that you don't want them to be too obvious. If your subject is a clock, for example, and your first line is:

I go tick tock

your riddle will lack mystery.

Riddles are older than history. They're a tantalizing, fascinating way of playing with language and ideas. Whether you're just reading the riddles in this collection to yourself, or trying them out on other people, or creating your own... Happy Riddling!

1

When you go faster
so do I
thumping like a drum
in my dark red cave.
When I stop
you will.

2

This is not a piece of
pretty lace
where rain and dew-
drops fall
and find their place
I made this silver veil
as light as breath
to be an instrument of
death.

3

Naked I walk
cold and naked
through the fields
I walk
that you may walk
warm.

4

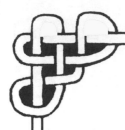

That wicked queen
she killed them both
the Bishop said
no prayer.
Behind his castle wall
the king
watched his mate
come near.
They view the battle
from afar
the stallion
and the mare.

5

Remember me
I never see
the sunlight shining
in the sky.
I do not sway
when breezes play
or watch the birds
take off and fly.
I toil and toil
down in the soil
beyond all season
sight and sound.
Remember me
oh mighty tree
your other half
beneath the ground.

6

I am complete
unto myself
but I am incomplete
without my partner.
We will travel
with you
until we can go
no further.

7

I show you the world
and sometimes
I show you yourself
you look
through yourself
at the world
the world looks
through me
at you.

8

I tell the world
that you were here.
Sometimes I'm hard to
see
sometimes I'm clear.
I show your skip
your jump
your run
and when the rain
descends
I'm quickly gone.

9

In the kettle
In the sky
In the rooftops
as they dry
In your breath
on mornings cold
Moonlit silver
Sunlit gold.

10

What I create
destroys me
What I uphold
wears me down
As your years pass
there are more of me
I rise like you
from darkness
like you
I return to it.

11

Here is a flat hill
here is a river
you can burn
here is a city
you can cover with
your thumb
here is a forest
whose color never
changes

A fly has landed
in the middle
of the sea.

12

I am earth
I am water
fire gives me strength
I hold earth
I hold water
beauty rises from me.

13

Inside outside
it's the same
How many of me
in my name?
See me flying
far and near
Touch me
and I disappear.

14

For this I came
for this I was fashioned
was given strength
and curving thin-walled
form
to shield and protect
a life
that will destroy me.

15

You give me breath.
you give me life.
If you give me
too much
I die.

16

Across me
the long wind whirls
Around me curl
the claws of birds
Within me flow
your distant words.

17

I know no words
and yet you speak
to me.
I know no music
and yet you sing to me.
I am a stranger
and yet you love me.

18

I am a man
without bones
my flesh is white.

I am a man
without blood
my flesh is cold.

I am a man
without life
my flesh is shrinking.

I am the man
you made and lost.

19

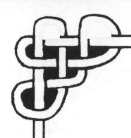

Each year
the pattern grows.
Another circle
forms within me.
Please wait
until the growing stops
before you cut.

20

For this was I made
for this
long have I
been dreaming.
I fling myself
into the sky
above the trees and
roofs I fly
and then I pause
and burst
and die
in colors bright
and gleaming.

21

You know me well
you trust me
as a friend
although you
never see me
never touch or taste
or talk to me.
When we are together
you do not know
that I am here
Without me
you cannot live for
long.

Look up at me
I am rising through air
I am flying.
Look up at me
I am riding on wind
I am dancing in space
as no bird can dance.
Look up at me
I am diving and rising
I am swooping and
looping
I am flying above you
high in the blue
of the sky.

Please let me go.
I want to be free.
I want to be free.

23

The more I eat
the greater is my
hunger.
I am appetite
I am need
I always want more
I ravage the land
like a roaring giant
that swells as it feeds.
If you see me coming
go where there is
nothing
for nothing stops me.

24

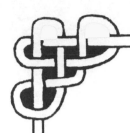

My body is long
my head is a clump
of stiff strong stalks.
Every morning
and every evening
I wear a soft hat
I enter the cave
and dance across
white stones
making them sparkle.

25

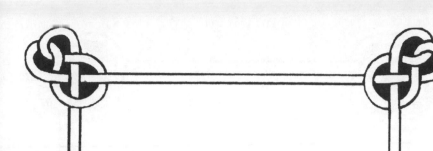

I fall
and I fall
and I fall

and I stay where I am

One-hole has no
patience
with other one-holes
He likes the two-holes
he flows into them
like an endless
stream.
Sometimes the two-
holes
close on either side of
him
would like other one-
holes
to flow into them
but this doesn't
happen very often.

27

No one belongs to us.
We do not glitter
on a lady's ring.
We do not beat
like a steady drum
We do not dig holes
in the ground.
There is no throne
there is no crown
there is no beanstalk.
But if you listen hard
you may hear the
sounds of laughter.

28

If you look at me
I remain as I am.
If you hold me
I return
to what I was.

29

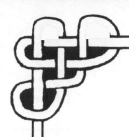

Clear and flowing
enters clear and still
and is still.
Clear and flowing
disappears
clear and still
is still there.

30

Summer follows me
north
then south.
My name
is in your mouth.

31

The sky is below me
I enter it.
My head is below me
I enter it.

32

You go under me
you go over me
at times you linger
on me
and look down
at yourself
looking up.

People gave me to you
mostly without
knowing
that they gave.
You keep me
and you pass me on to
others.

Use me as you wish.
Once you know
the rules
there are no rules
except your own.

I am the door
in every wall
I am the bridge
between each island
I am what you see
or hear
right now
at this very moment.

34

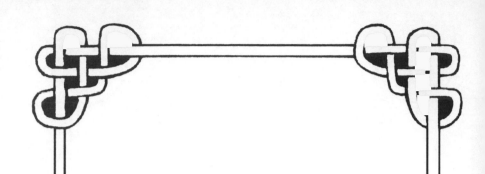

There are not many of
us.
You can touch us all
with your fingers
But we can go further
then you can see
or think.
We can make a line
whose ending
you will never find.

35

I show you the sun
then I show you
the moon
then I show you
the wind

and then I start
all over again

36

Fight for me
hold me
die with me

37

If you can hear
where I come from
I am no longer there.

Riddle Solutions:

1 - Heart
2 - Spider's web
3 -Sheep
4 - Chess
5 - Tree roots
6 - Shoes
7 - Window
8 - Footprints
9 - Clouds or steam
10- Birthday Candles
11 - Map
12 - Flower Pot
13 - Bubbles
14- Egg
15- Balloon or Bubble
16 - Telephone wire
17 - Baby
18 - Snowman
19 - Tree Rings
20- Rocket
21- Sleep
22 - Kite
23 - Fire
24 - Toothbrush
25 - Waterfall
26 - Mouth and Ears
27 - Playing cards
28 - Ice or Snow
29- Glass of Water
30 - Swallow
31- Waterbird
32- Bridge
33- Language
34 - Numbers, or digits
35- Dandelion
36 - Breath
37 - Seashell

TEACHERS' NOTES - RIDDLE WRITING

Riddles are particularly enjoyed by students grades 5 to 8, although older students - and adults - also like the challenge they present.

They have a long history in the world's oral tradition, from the riddle of the sphinx to Gollum's riddles in The Hobbit. The riddles in this collection are based on early English riddles - mystifying poems describing people or objects. The Exeter Book of Riddles served as a model for me; riddles in which the subject of the riddle describes itself, as in this riddle about a swan:

Silent is my dress when I step across the earth,
reside in my house, or ruffle the waters.
Sometimes my adornments and this high windy air
lift me over the livings of men;
the power of the clouds carries me far
over all people. My white pinions
resound very loudly, ring with a melody
sing out clearly, when I sleep not on
the soil or settle on gray waters - a travelling spirit.

The riddles in 'Man without Bones' are written quite consciously in a number of styles. Some have a rhyme scheme and a regular structure; some are free verse; some are quite short and plain, others are more poetic in their use of language. My intention was to create a collection that showed students a wide range of poetic writing, partly to enrich their understanding of poetry, and also so that they have a greater range of options when they write their own.

The collection is organized so that the easier riddles are at the beginning, and get harder as the book progresses. Once students understand how they work - and, in my experience, they get the hang of this quite quickly - they get very involved in the process of pondering on the details each riddles gives them and waiting for that intuitive flash that provides the answer. I've kept to subjects that are more or less universally familiar, so that the riddles can work with anybody, anywhere. Sometimes, if students are stuck, I provide clues - a short phrase pointing them in a particular direction, or a quick mime. "Think winter." "It's a kind of plant."

RUNNING A RIDDLE-WRITING WORKSHOP

After reading a number of riddles I suggest that the students write their own. By this time they've invariably got caught up in the challenge that riddles present, and are eager to compose their own.

The basic point to get across is that these riddles are something or somebody speaking, without telling us what or who they are. You have to get inside the skin of something or someone else and allow it, him or her speak through you. Riddles should be written so that there are enough details to make them solvable, but not so that they are EASILY solvable. A riddle that's obvious simply doesn't work. Also, riddles about subjects that very few people know about - for example, an expensive video game - don't work. It's better to choose a subject that everyone is familiar with. I often do a group riddle with the class; we agree on a subject then I write lines - or clues - on the board as the students dictate them. This is a better way to explain the rules, or principles, of riddling than dry exposition.

For example, we might pick 'a clock' as a subject. (There's usually one in the classroom). If a student suggests: 'I go tick tock', then the solution is obvious, therefore the riddle doesn't work. You then have students thinking hard about a very ordinary object and looking for ways to describe it that are interesting and enigmatic, or mysterious. "I have hands but I touch nothing.... I am always traveling but I never arrive..." This, I believe, is an excellent language and thinking problem to set them.

Encourage the students to create riddles that are interesting not only as verbal puzzles, but in the way they use language. The ideal riddle is a good puzzle AND a good poem. Encourage them to use simile and metaphor. (The toothbrush riddle is a good example of this - the toothpaste is a soft hat, the mouth is a cave, the teeth are white stones.) Or to try a parallel or repeated structure, like the snowman riddle. I often pin up or write on the chalkboard a list of riddle subjects for those students who find it difficult to get started. I've included this list for you to use if you wish.

Because riddles are usually quite short, students will often write 2 or 3. They'll eagerly try them out an each other, and on the teacher. It's a good idea to keep some time back before the end of the lesson so that students can read their riddles to the class. The riddles can be printed out and then either put up in a display, or put together in a book, so that students from other classes can try solving them.

Riddles are a lot of fun. As a poet who visits schools I have never known them to fail. I often get kids I taught them to coming up to me in the street or the supermarket weeks later, asking me to say a riddle or wanting to tell me one they wrote after my visit. They appeal to our love of puzzles, of playing with words, of creating challenges for one another. They're a precious part of our oral tradition, an ancient form of language play that deserves to be revived. I hope you get as much pleasure out of teaching them as I do.

Note: The Exeter Book of Riddles I have is in Penguin Classics, translated by Kevin Crossley-Holland. Many of the riddles it contains are mere fragments, and are therefore unusable in a classroom setting. The introduction, however, offers an excellent brief history of riddles which you may find useful.

Emmanuel Williams

RIDDLE SUBJECTS

Pencil * Ball * Rose * Computer * Dream * Car * Rainbow * Mouse * Worm * Phone * Tattoo * Camera * Moon * Drum * Belt * Skin * Eyes * TV * Candle * Clock * Fog * Cloud * Glasses * Mirror * Bed * Hand * Chair * Scissors * Calendar * Classroom * Water * Thunder * Stomach * Traffic-light * Bell * Parents * Fish * Unicorn * Gun * wing * Snake * Lipstick * Shower * Cow * Comb * Bike * Ladder * Aquarium * Apple * Bee * Match * Name * Door * Hair * Teeth * Snake * Photograph * Caterpillar * Volcano * Sky * Bath * Flea * Phone * Riddle

QUIDDLES

(Quiddles are quick concentrated riddles based on rhyming. If you like word patterns you may enjoy creating your own quiddles.)

1	2	3	4
sow	gold	white	lake
grow	band	flight	bait
mow	hold	wish	wait
dough	hand	fish	take
	kiss		
	bliss		

5	6	7	8
high	bars	skilled	crawl
eye	wait	build	soil
hover	key	blast	hole
over	years	fast	hill
drop	gate	fly	
stop	free	sky	
kill			
fill			

9	10	11
tree	thin	thin
growth	skin	in
red	round	finger
me	sound	ouch
mouth		out
fed		better

QUIDDLE SOLUTIONS:

1 – Bread
2 – Wedding
3 – Gull
4 – Fishing
5 – Hawk
6 - Jail
7 – Rocket
8 – Mole
9 – Apple
10 – Drum
11 - Splinter